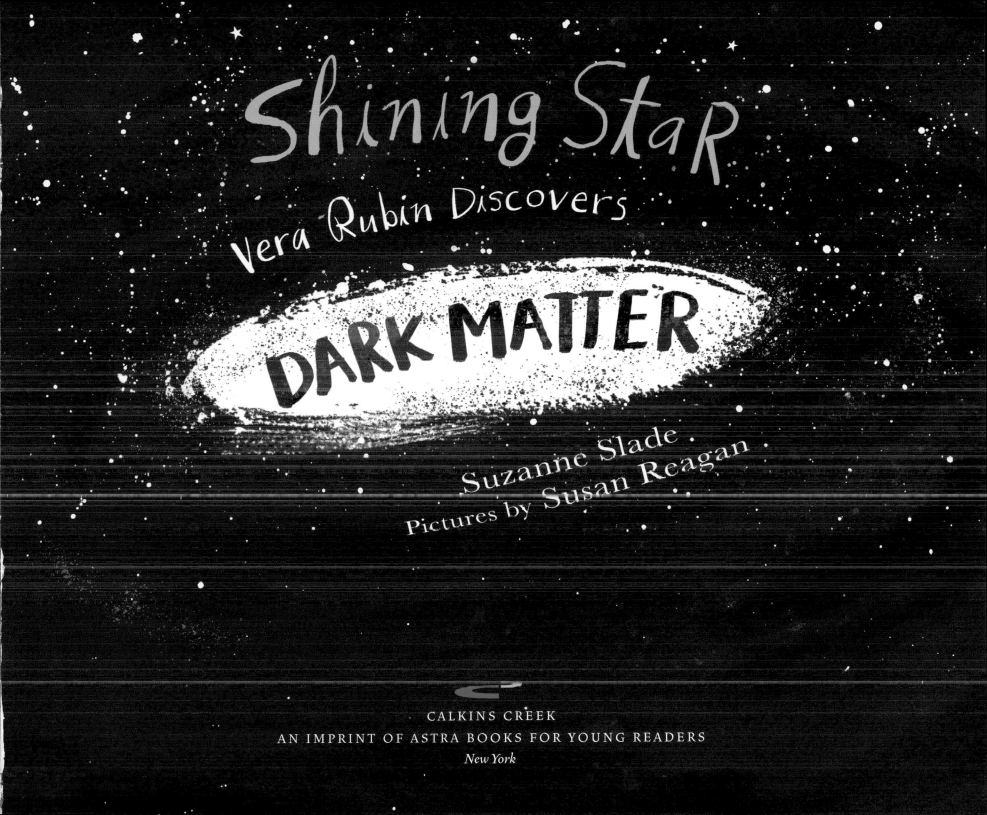

Shining Star

Vera Rubin Discovers

DARK MATTER

Suzanne Slade

Pictures by Susan Reagan

CALKINS CREEK

AN IMPRINT OF ASTRA BOOKS FOR YOUNG READERS

New York

On a dark, cloudless night, tiny pinpoints of light shone bright in Vera's window.

Curious, she leaned outside, turned her face toward the sky, and sighed.

Vera was plumb starstruck!

"We live in a fascinatingly beautiful universe."

Vera liked many things.

The smell of new books at the library. The dancing colors in her kaleidoscope. The majestic songs at Saturday temple.

She even liked her annoying sister (well, most of the time).

But Vera ADORED stars!

"There was just nothing as interesting in my life as watching the stars every night."

"I would prefer to stay up and watch the stars than go to sleep."

Vera studied how those twinkles of light slowly slid across the sky.

She memorized the names of constellations.

Sometimes, she stayed up all night considering colossal, cosmic questions:

Why did stars travel along curved paths?

How did people tell time by watching stars move?

Why did different stars appear in different seasons?

"From about the age of ten, I knew I wanted to be an astronomer."

Vera longed for a closer look at the sparkling stars. So she built a telescope, with her father's help, from a cardboard tube and a glass lens she ordered through the mail.

Peering at those distant shimmering lights, Vera had a stellar idea. She would become a professional stargazer—an astronomer!

Vera's out-of-sight obsession exploded.

She joined an astronomy club. She drew maps of marvelous meteor showers. She learned how to photograph stars streaking through the sky. Even her high school English papers were about telescopes!

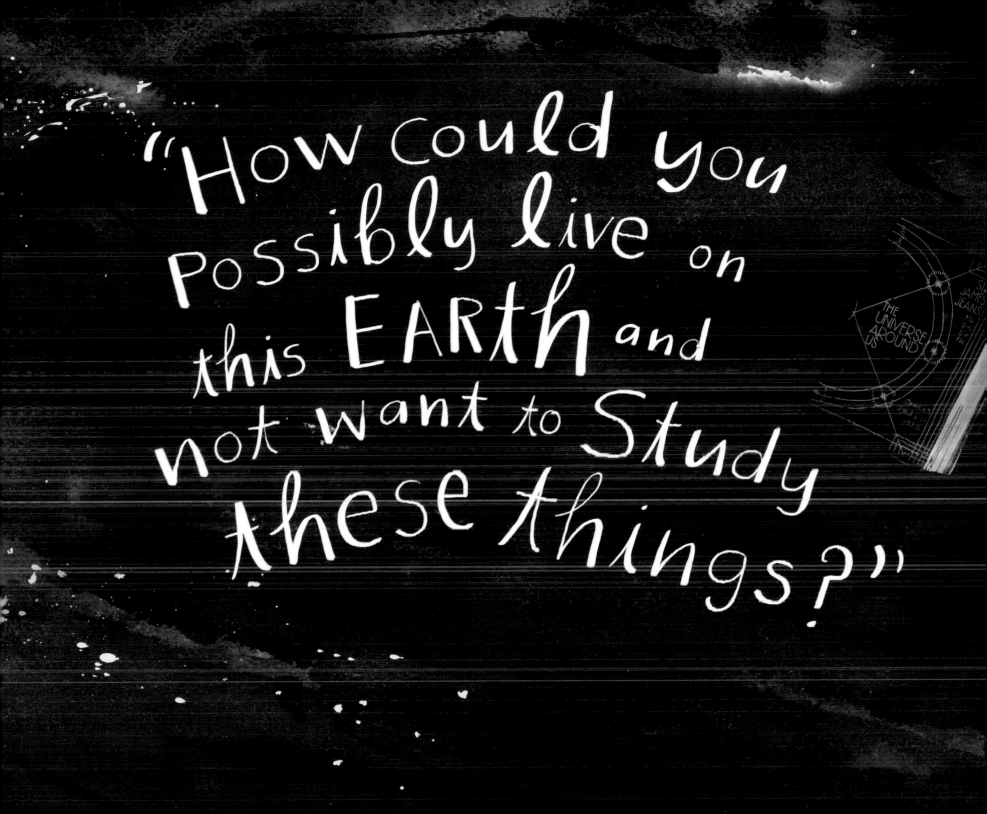

Vera soon discovered her far-out career path wasn't going to be easy. Few colleges allowed women to study astronomy. Determined, she applied to three schools that did.

Vassar College offered her a scholarship. When she announced the news to her science teacher (who said only boys should be scientists), he replied, "As long as you stay away from science, you should do okay."

But Vera didn't!

"I was never discouraged by others who were sometimes discouraging."

THE REALM OF THE
NEBULÆ

BY EDWIN HUBBLE

ASTRONOMY

Sperical Astronomy
W.M. Smart
Pages: 442 (English)

Like a shooting star, Vera soared through college. She studied
giant galaxies filled with billions of stars. At graduation, she
was the only astronomy student in the class.

Stars in her eyes, Vera went on to Cornell University for a
master's degree in astronomy. The classes were tough.
Astrochemistry. Quantum electrodynamics. And galaxy dynamics.
But she was tougher, and whip-smart too!

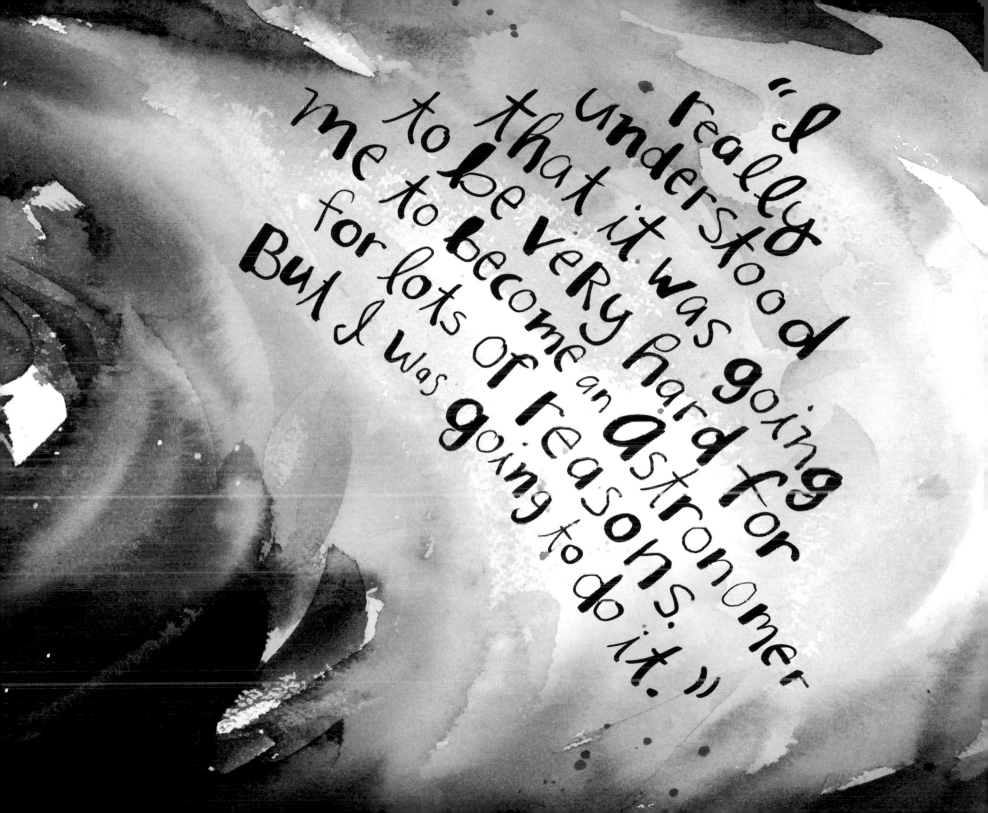

"I really understood that it was going to be very hard for me to become an astronomer for lots of reasons. But I was going to do it."

Next, she attended Georgetown University and earned a PhD in astronomy and became *Dr.* Vera Rubin!

Vera began teaching, but she also kept her eyes on the sky.

To study stars, she needed access to huge observatory telescopes. Men were given top priority to use them. So Vera had to wait. And wait.

When observatories finally offered her time, she traveled long distances to visit them.

She trudged up Kitt Peak in Arizona to observe stars circling in our Milky Way Galaxy.

She hiked up to the McDonald Observatory dome in Texas to search for far-off galaxies.

Vera's love for galaxies was so astronomical, she took a job at the Carnegie Institution in Washington, DC, to research them full-time. There she met Dr. Kent Ford and his spectacular spectrograph. When attached to a telescope, his device created images that showed how stars moved.

Vera and Kent lugged the new spectrograph to Arizona to test it. (Actually, Vera was more excited about studying galaxies.) First, she used a finding chart to locate a certain star. Then she pointed the telescope and spectrograph toward that spot. As the star moved, Vera guided the telescope to follow it.

Lowell Observatory

ROUTE
66

Captivated by these celestial sights, Vera dreamed of the powerful telescopes on Palomar Mountain in California. But that observatory had a strict policy: no women.

Vera wanted to change that rule. So she filled out a form to observe there (even though it said, "It is not possible to accept applications from women").

Scientists at Palomar knew Vera was an out-of-this-world astronomer. And just like that, their "rule" vanished.

ELEVATION
5550 FT

"We all need permission to do Science, but, for reasons that are deeply ingrained in history, this permission is more often given to men than to women."

On a cold December night, Vera became the first woman allowed to observe at Palomar. The starry view through their 48-inch telescope was stupendous!

But the building was not. There was only one bathroom—for men.

Of course, Vera later solved that problem. She drew a picture of a woman wearing a skirt and stuck it on the door!

After years of research, Vera turned her focus to spiral galaxies. She wanted to learn how stars revolve around the center of a spiral galaxy. Vera decided to start with a nearby galaxy named Andromeda and its one trillion twinkling star lights. Vera and Kent headed back to Arizona to study Andromeda.

At the US Naval Observatory, the night air was freezing cold. The two took turns guiding the telescope, while the other huddled near a heater.

At Kitt Peak Observatory, waves of blistering heat rolled off the desert sand all night. But Vera stayed cool by devouring ice-cream cones.

Those twelve-hour night shifts were long, but to Vera, the hours seemed to fly. She was racing the Sun! As soon as it peeked over the horizon, her precious viewing time was over.

"During that time of darkness, each minute will be precious, and I will be aware that I am racing the Sun."

When Vera gathered her results of Andromeda's swirling stars, she was puzzled.

Astronomers believed stars on the outer edge of a spiral galaxy moved slower than stars near the center. But her results showed all of Andromeda's stars were traveling at about the same speed!

Vera studied dozens more spiral galaxies. Her findings didn't change. Stars on the outside of a galaxy moved at the same velocity as stars near the center!

Astronomers around the world shook their heads. *Preposterous!* Everyone knew stars in a galaxy behaved like planets in the solar system. Objects near the outside orbited more slowly than those closer to the center.

Yet Vera knew her results were correct. She also knew something was pulling on the stars and affecting their speed. Something invisible. *But what?*

Vera studied more spiral galaxies.
Finally, she figured out the answer could only be
one thing—a mysterious material scientists had wondered
about for years. Dark matter!
Dark matter didn't shine like stars.
It wasn't visible like planets.
And no one had evidence it existed. Until now.

"We have peered into a new World and have Seen that it is more Mysterious and More Complex than we had imagined."

Vera realized dark matter was spread out all over a galaxy. Her stunning discovery helped astronomers understand something their eyes couldn't see—the universe contained more dark matter than anything.

And this dark matter was pulling on stars. It was holding all the galaxies—the entire universe—together!

"Still more Mysteries of the universe remain hidden," Vera announced.

"What keeps me going is this hope and curiosity, this basic curiosity about how the universe works."

AUTHOR'S NOTE

A picture book is a great way to introduce people of all ages to inspiring figures like Dr. Rubin. For curious readers, here's a bit more about this pioneering astronomer.

Vera Rubin, age 14, with her homemade telescope, 1942

Vera's father, Philip, was a Jewish immigrant from Lithuania. He excelled at math and earned an electrical engineering degree from the University of Pennsylvania.

Vera's mother, Rose, was born in the United States to two Jewish immigrants from Europe. Rose met Philip at Bell Telephone Company where they both worked. The two married, and before long Vera was born in Philadelphia. When Vera was ten, her family moved to Washington, DC. While gazing through her bedroom window, Vera was captivated by the stars. Her parents supported her curiosity about astronomy. Her mother wrote a note to the librarian giving permission for Vera to check out science books from the adult section. Vera's father helped her build a telescope and accompanied Vera to amateur astronomer club meetings.

After graduating with a bachelor's degree from Vassar College, Vera married Robert Rubin in 1948. Although she was devoted to research, spending time with her husband was a top priority. Through the years, they added four children to their family.

Dr. Rubin began her career at Montgomery County Junior College where she taught for a year. Then she moved on to Georgetown University and taught there for ten years while doing research. In 1965 she accepted a position at Carnegie Institution's Department of Terrestrial Magnetism and began studying the motion of stars and distribution of mass in spiral galaxies. She collaborated with Dr. Kent Ford from Carnegie, as well as other astronomers.

Studying galaxies was tedious work. First, Dr. Rubin used a map of stars called a finding chart to locate a star she wanted to study. She often attached an image tube on a telescope that amplified faint starlight to help her see distant stars better. Dr. Ford's spectrograph allowed her to determine the speed of moving stars. To understand how it worked, consider the way

Vera Rubin at Vassar College telescope, 1948

raindrops separate sunlight into different colors of a rainbow. Similarly, the spectrograph separated light from a star into its component colors, and recorded them on a small, glass plate. Using those images, Dr. Rubin calculated how fast stars were moving. Her discoveries about the star speeds in spiral galaxies provided solid evidence that dark matter exists.

But Dr. Rubin's contributions to science go beyond her

research. She worked hard to help women obtain equal opportunities in scientific fields. She encouraged girls to start studying science and math in elementary school. When she met women science students in college who were frustrated by inequalities, Vera firmly admonished them, "Don't quit." She fought discrimination against women wherever it appeared, such as in all-male faculty departments or conferences which only invited male speakers, and continually urged the science community to "offer women a warm welcome in science."

In honor of Dr. Rubin's work, the asteroid 5726 Rubin was named after her. She is memorialized with Vera Rubin Ridge on Mars. The National Science Foundation Vera C. Rubin Observatory in Chile was the first national US observatory named after a woman astronomer. Her accomplishments were also recognized with numerous honors including the US National Medal of Science, the Gold Medal of the Royal Astronomical Society in London, the Gruber Foundation Cosmology Prize, the James Craig Watson Medal of the US National Academy of Sciences, and various honorary degrees.

Many astronomy experts feel that Dr. Rubin should have earned a Nobel Prize in Physics for her dark matter research, but was overlooked because she was a woman. This esteemed award is only given to scientists who are living, so when she died in 2016, the dream that she would be recognized with this prestigious award ended too.

Although Dr. Rubin did not win a Nobel Prize for her incredible discoveries, she received another prize—happiness. As Dr. Rubin shared, "Successful nights at a telescope are among the happiest nights of my life."

DR. RUBIN'S DARK MATTER DISCOVERY

Our solar system contains eight planets all orbiting around the Sun. The planet closest to the Sun, Mercury, travels the fastest. The farther a planet is from the Sun, the slower its orbital velocity. Why? The Sun's huge mass creates a gravitational field that pulls on the planets and affects their speed.

Vera Rubin works with a telescope at Lowell Observatory in 1965.

For decades astronomers thought spiral galaxies worked the same way. A spiral galaxy is made up of billions of stars orbiting around its bright center called a bulge. That bulge is actually a group of stars packed closely together. Due to the gravitational pull created by a bulge's mighty mass, scientists believed that stars located farther from the center of the galaxy would orbit more slowly than those closer to the center.

When Vera announced her discovery "that stars very far from the centers of their galaxies were orbiting with very high velocities," scientists were stunned! At first, Vera didn't know why stars on the outside of galaxies moved faster than expected

Vera Rubin looks into a spectrograph at Kitt Peak 1965.

(about the same speed as other stars in the galaxy). The concept of an invisible matter that held galaxies together had been suggested by astronomer Fritz Zwicky in the 1930s. Most scientists back then ignored his idea, and so did later astronomers. But after further research, Vera realized the stars she'd been studying were "responding to the gravitational field of matter which we don't see." She was the first to provide strong, concrete evidence for dark matter! No one knows exactly what dark matter is, but we do know there is more of it than the matter we can see. Scientists also believe dark matter creates a gravitational pull that acts like "glue" and holds the universe together. Today, scientists continue to build off of Vera's groundbreaking work as they strive to better understand mysterious dark matter.

TIMELINE

1928 Vera Florence Cooper is born on July 23 in Philadelphia.

1939 Vera's family moves to Washington, DC.

1948 She graduates from Vassar College with a bachelor's degree in astronomy.

1948 Vera marries Robert Rubin on June 25.

1950 First child, David, is born.

1951 Vera is awarded a master's degree in astronomy by Cornell University.

1952 Daughter Judith is born.

1954 Dr. Rubin completes her PhD in astronomy at Georgetown University.

1954–55 She works as a math and physics instructor at Montgomery County Junior College.

1955–65 Dr. Rubin is a researcher, lecturer, and assistant professor at Georgetown University.

1956 Son Karl is born.

1960 Son Allan is born.

1965 She begins working at the Carnegie Institution's Department of Terrestrial Magnetism as a staff scientist, and meets Dr. Kent Ford there.

1965 Dr. Rubin is the first woman granted permission to observe at Palomar Observatory in Southern California.

1968 She decides to focus her research on the Andromeda Galaxy (M31).

1970 Dr. Rubin and Dr. Ford's article about star movement in the Andromeda Galaxy, "Rotation of the Andromeda Nebula from a Spectroscopic Survey of Emission Regions," is published in *The Astrophysical Journal*.

1979 Dr. Rubin and Dr. Ford announce their conclusion that dark matter exists in the *Carnegie Institution Year Book 78* (1978–79).

1981 Dr. Rubin is admitted into the National Academy of Sciences.

1983 *Science* publishes Dr. Rubin's article, "The Rotation of Spiral Galaxies," which shares evidence that orbital velocities of stars in galaxies confirm the existence of dark matter.

1993 President Bill Clinton awards Dr. Rubin the National Medal of Science.

1996 Dr. Rubin's book, *Bright Galaxies, Dark Matters* is published.

2016 Dr. Vera Cooper Rubin passes away on December 25.

The Andromeda Galaxy, a spiral galaxy that Dr. Rubin studied

SELECTED BIBLIOGRAPHY*

All quotations used in the book can be found in the following sources marked with an asterisk (*).

BOOKS

* Rubin, Vera. *Bright Galaxies, Dark Matters.* New York: Springer-Verlag, 1996.

JOURNAL, MAGAZINE, AND NEWSPAPER ARTICLES

Overbye, Dennis. "Vera Rubin, 88, Dies; Opened Doors in Astronomy, and for Women." *New York Times*, December 27, 2016. nytimes.com/2016/12/27/science/vera-rubin-astronomist-who-made-the-case-for-dark-matter-dies-at-88.html.

Rubin, Vera. "Fluctuations in the Space Distribution of the Galaxies." *Proceedings of the National Academy of Sciences* 40, no. 7 (1954): 541–9.

———. "An Interesting Voyage." *Annual Review of Astronomy and Astrophysics*, 2011: 1–28. annualreviews.org/doi/full/10.1146/annurev-astro-081710-102545.

———. "The Rotation of Spiral Galaxies." *Science* 220, no. 4604 (1983): 1339–1344. science.sciencemag.org/content/220/4604/1339.

Scoles, Sarah. "How Vera Rubin Confirmed Dark Matter." *Astronomy*, October 4, 2016. astronomy.com/news/2016/10/vera-rubin.

INTERVIEWS WITH VERA RUBIN

* Interview by David DeVorkin. Niels Bohr Library & Archives, American Institute of Physics, College Park, Maryland, September 21, 1995. aip.org/history-programs/niels-bohr-library/oral-histories/5920-1.

———. Niels Bohr Library & Archives, American Institute of Physics, College Park, Maryland, May 9, 1996. aip.org/history-programs/niels-bohr-library/oral-histories/5920-2.

* Interview by Alan Lightman. Niels Bohr Library & Archives, American Institute of Physics, College Park, Maryland, April 3, 1989. aip.org/history-programs/niels-bohr-library/oral-histories/33963.

WEBSITES**

Carnegie Science. "Kent Ford & Vera Rubin's Image Tube Spectrograph named in Smithsonian's 101 Objects that Made America,'" November 4, 2013. dtm.carnegiescience.edu/news/kent-ford-vera-rubins-image-tube-spectrograph-named-smithsonians-101-objects-made-america.

University of California, Los Angeles. Contributions of 20th Century Women to Physics. "Rubin, Vera Cooper." cwp.library.ucla.edu/Phase2/Rubin,_Vera_Cooper@931234567.html.

**Websites active at time of publication

ACKNOWLEDGMENTS

The author is deeply grateful to Shaun Hardy, librarian at the Carnegie Institution for Science, Washington, DC, for answering many questions, vetting the manuscript, and assisting with photo research. Also, sincere thanks to Eve Chase, PhD in astronomy, currently at Los Alamos National Laboratory in New Mexico, and Candice Stauffer, PhD student, astronomy, Northwestern University, for sharing their expertise and reviewing the story for accuracy.

Vera Rubin measures galaxy spectra at the Department of Terrestrial Magnetism, Carnegie Institution, 1972.

To my PWIDDY Committee shining stars: Deborah Topolski, Sara Shacter, Alice McGinty, Lisa Bierman, Natalie Rompella, Lori Degman, Patty Toht, Darcy Zoells, Janet McDonnell, Terri Murphy, Meg Fleming Lentz, and Laura Crawford —*SS*

For all my beautiful nieces. Go girl power! —*SR*

For information about permission to reproduce selections from this book, please contact permissions@astrapublishinghouse.com.

Calkins Creek
An imprint of Astra Books for Young Readers, a division of Astra Publishing House
astrapublishinghouse.com
Printed in China

ISBN: 978-1-63592-601-9 (hc)
ISBN: 978-1-63592-602-6 (eBook)
Library of Congress Control Number: 2022949588

First edition
10 9 8 7 6 5 4 3 2 1

Design by Barbara Grzeslo
The text is set in Futura Std Medium.
The illustrations are created with hand-painted watercolor washes and ink lines that are combined and enhanced digitally in Photoshop.